HOW TO CREATE A CRAPPY BRAND*
IN 3 EASY STEPS

Using clichés to convey brand value and distinction

Me-too messaging

Useless crud

CRAP

Copying what other brands are doing to steer what your brand is doing

Mindless waste

Seeking advice of mother/spouse/ next door neighbor/ dog about what your brand <u>should</u> be doing

*SOMETHING THIS BOOK HELPS YOU AVOID

BRAND INTER-VENTION

33 STEPS TO TRANSFORM THE BRAND YOU HAVE INTO THE BRAND YOU NEED

DAVID BRIER

BRAND INTERVENTION
33 Steps to Transform the Brand You Have into the Brand You Need

Visit the author's website at **www.RisingAboveTheNoise.com** and **www.BrandInterventionBook.com** for new updates and Brand Intervention exclusives.

ISBN 978-0-9995297-0-6 (Hardcover)
ISBN 978-0-9995297-1-3 (Softcover)
ISBN 978-0-9995297-2-0 (E-book)

Publisher: DBD International, Ltd.

Author/Designer: David Brier

Editor: Patricia Ross

Interior Layout: Ronda Taylor

"Please remain seated until the ride
has come to a complete stop."
Roller coaster loudspeaker

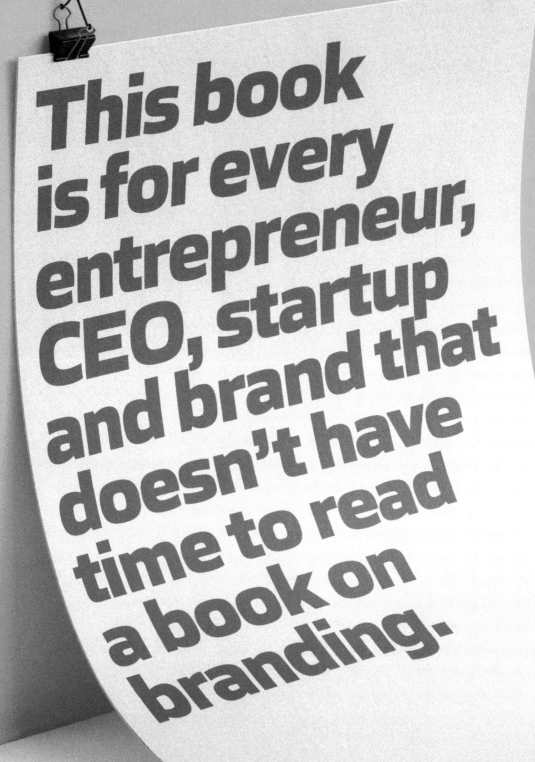

This book is for every entrepreneur, CEO, startup and brand that doesn't have time to read a book on branding.

Contents

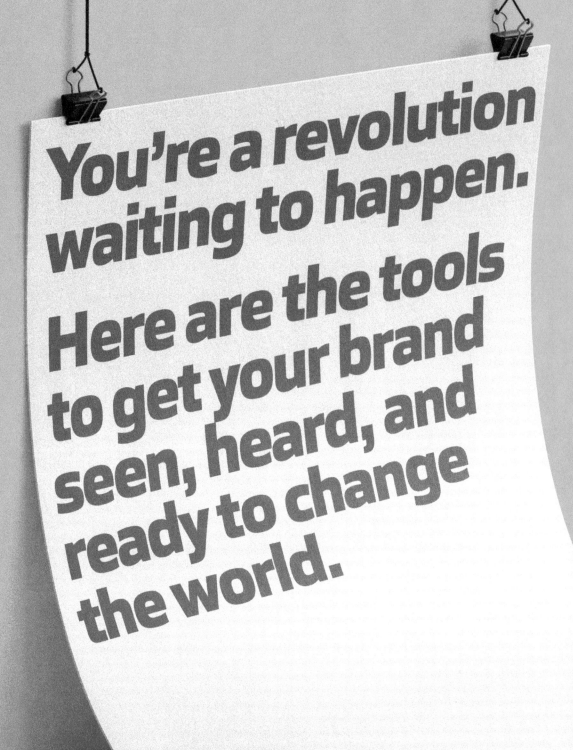

"You don't have to have money to brand as David will show you. It's a mentality. It's actually acting like you don't have any money and forcing creativity, exercising what I call 'The Power of Broke.'"
Daymond John

Foreword
by Daymond John

I know from personal experience, if you didn't brand, you were nothing.

If you didn't innovate, you were dead.

If you didn't approach business with the hunger and drive of an entrepreneur, you were broke.

If I didn't do those three things in my career, I wouldn't have gotten to where I am today. I apply them as much today as I did when I first started.

Many years after those early days in my career, I was commenting on a pitch given on *Shark Tank* and said something to the effect of, there are two types of people in the world: Sharks and wannabe Sharks.

Which is why this book on *Brand Intervention* connected with me so much. It's the intervening between merely having things happen versus *making* things happen.

The Worst Thing in Business

The worst thing I see (whether it's in the *Tank* or any other time I'm reviewing a business opportunity) is someone who doesn't know how to connect the dots, who doesn't know the proper way to plot out their career and create their future history, or know the proven mindset that will help separate the good from the bad and the ugly.

When I started my career that ultimately became the fashion empire of FUBU with only a handful of shirts (while still working at Red Lobster), I would have benefitted from having the tips and insights found in this book. I would've likely made some different and more informed choices (saving me time and money in the long run).

I was fortunate to be raised by my single mother who intuitively knew early on I would never fit into the "corporate machine" and was by nature an entrepreneur. She was right.

Thankfully, my mother (who was my inspiration) was also a fighter who never quit even if it meant having three jobs to keep it all together. She did everything possible to raise me with integrity and accountability. She made sure I was surrounded by inspiring mentors, so I learned to find value in others and their knowledge.

She had an amazing instinct for this thing called "entrepreneurship" many years before I even knew what that word meant.

She also knew about innovation and goals and had an innate sense that "you had to stand for something" (which is her way of talking about branding).

So when David told me of his new book about *Brand Intervention*, I had to write the Foreword.

Why?

Because there are too few books that talk about how to create a a future as an entrepreneur. Like, "How do you really envision and create a future?" and "What's the difference between CEOs who 'get it' and other business leaders who don't, merely relying on old, tired solutions?" (Plus I've been a fan of David's intelligent posts for *Fast Company* and articles featuring him in *Forbes, INC.*, and others.)

That's what this book does.

It outlines key milestones and signposts every successful business I know uses to map their way to creating businesses, niches, brands, growth, and wealth others overlook or simply don't recognize.

Read this book to connect the dots others miss.

Daymond John
@theSharkDaymond
#powerofbroke

Brands can no longer just "get by."

Brands today must be relevant, distinct, real, definitive, and not entirely predictable.

Anything less demands an intervention.

This book reveals the mindset required to successfully correct a brand that's made wrong choices.

"The key to generating loyalty and rising above the general noise seems to be all about creating an authentic voice."

Richard Branson, English business entrepreneur and investor

Introduction

Why I wrote this book

If you've ever doubted your ability to successfully disrupt an industry, this book will help you.

If you've ever wondered what all those branding and marketing theories mean, this book cuts right through that noise and shows you how to avoid the potholes and defy the odds.

If you've ever felt some people and brands are just plain lucky, this book can turn that around.

For over 30 years, clients have faced branding problems and asked me the same questions, no matter their industry.

While I take the same strategic approach and analysis no matter the industry, each client's brand ends up unique, sounding and looking distinct and memorable. Yet they share the same foundational principles needed to stand apart and get noticed.

Clients are all convinced their problems are unusual or uncommon. To a certain extent, they are. But they look in all the wrong places to solve their issues.

I know where to look and, after reading this book, you will too.

I know the questions to ask and when to stop asking questions.

With this book, you can learn to as well. Some may get their feathers ruffled by you taking such a direct approach, but many more will respect you and have a newfound regard for your dogged persistence.

I've outlined the mindset needed to strip away this false notion: that a great brand or cause is reason enough to succeed.

It's not. That's Hollywood. Not real life.

There are too many crappy products that sell and too many great products that fail for anyone to insist on the "good karma" hypothesis.

Besides, too many brands think that.

Your competitors have the same idea of how unique, special, vital, and relevant they are with everyone spending a lot of money using the same words, messages, and promises to convince prospects how unique they each are.

Words are just one tool.

There are numerous other tools companies don't know how to use or haven't mastered. And I am not talking about "social media" as a tool. Social media is a distribution tool. I'm talking about design, color, imagery, typography, style and form (as in packaging).

Having branded global brands like Revlon, Estee Lauder and *Rolling Stone* magazine, I know the power of branding applied to these big brands. As a result, my clients' brands and their stories end up better than they could produce by themselves.

I've taken local brands like Legacy Chocolates in the Midwest and Botanical Bakery from Napa Valley, 3Xing sales in 30 days and 9Xing their sales in 24 months respectively.

All because the design, message, and brand "spoke" the right way. So I know this works for startups.

These same principles have even been applied to cities, increasing their tourism traffic as much as 500% in as little as 12 months.

Or a VIP brand like Joanna Vargas Salon in NYC, and helping them explode their company 800% with new clients in just a few months. So these intervention principles even work for niche boutique brands.

I know the magic that can occur and why intervention is necessary: because brands are too close to themselves to be objective. The result is too many brands functioning at a fraction of their capacity.

There's no reason and no excuse good enough to continue to do that anymore.

That's the power of *Brand Intervention,* and that's why I wrote this book.

David Brier

"One more thing..."
Steve Jobs

A 24/7 branding buffet

Brand Intervention is like an all-you-can-eat buffet, having two distinct parts. One part consists of short, actionable points—the exact points to stupid-proof you against "brand speak" and other bits of corporate stupidity.

No wasted words and zero waste of your time.

In other words, this is **not** a feel-good book.

It's an action book.

Without these actionable points understood and in place, nothing you do for your brand will matter. Zero.

That's part one.

Part two at the end of the book provides you eye candy and "fly-on-the-wall" insights into **how** to use these principles. These are in the "Brand Intervention Playbook" section of the book.

It's here you'll **see** befores and afters—actual interventions clients have gone through, transforming these hopeful and well-meaning brands into lean, mean branding machines.

Together, these two parts give you powerful insights and real-life examples of brands and their interventions.

Your brand deserves this.

Now, let's get this party started.

"Determine who you are and what your brand is, and what you're not. The rest of it is just a lot of noise."
Geoffrey Zakarian, Armenian-American Iron Chef, restaurateur, and author

1

The attention span of a goldfish

You don't have time to blow it.

A recent study (by Microsoft) discovered this startling fact: goldfish have an attention span of 9 seconds before flicking onto the next item.

We humans now have the attention span of 8 seconds compared to the 12-second attention span we allegedly used to possess.

That's right. One second less than a freaking goldfish.

At the same time, I discovered a disturbing fact: I went to Amazon and searched for books on the subject of branding.

The result was an astonishing 8,000+ books. Not on love, romance, wizards, or

Hollywood biographies but, of all things, branding!

In short, there's way too much complexity and theorizing on the topic and too little attention to sift through what's actually valuable to successfully take it all in.

Which brings us to this question: will your brand's message engage your audience in 8 seconds?

Or leave them drowning in a sea of marketing debris?

The greatest brands, entrepreneurs, and creators share one trait: they get very restless when things get too comfortable.

"It's not that you can't, it's that you're not willing to give up dumb shit for a better life."
Gary Vaynerchuk, American serial entrepreneur, four-time *NY Times* bestselling author, and speaker

2

Too many brands just show up

Culturally, we're in the
"I showed up" era where
businesses and people
think showing up (or taking
something to market) is
good enough.

It's not. No brand is "entitled"
to anything merely because
it has good intentions. That's
not the real world.

In part, that's due to the sheer amount of overused "promises" most businesses employ in their messages.

Great brands have wonderful things to convey compared to lousy brands. When lousy brands say "great service," it means something very different than when a great brand utters the same words.

The problem is: prospective customers end up hearing **the same words** we all use "to define how unique we are" when in fact we're each attempting to convey **very** different things.

Plus, too many of us have forgotten what's it like to excel.

Let's not forget the root word of **excellence** is excel. You don't achieve excellence by doing what's expected (or merely showing up). That's like celebrating every time you take your next breath. Definitely **not** the attitude necessary to create an amazing brand that truly inspires loyalty and ignites imaginations.

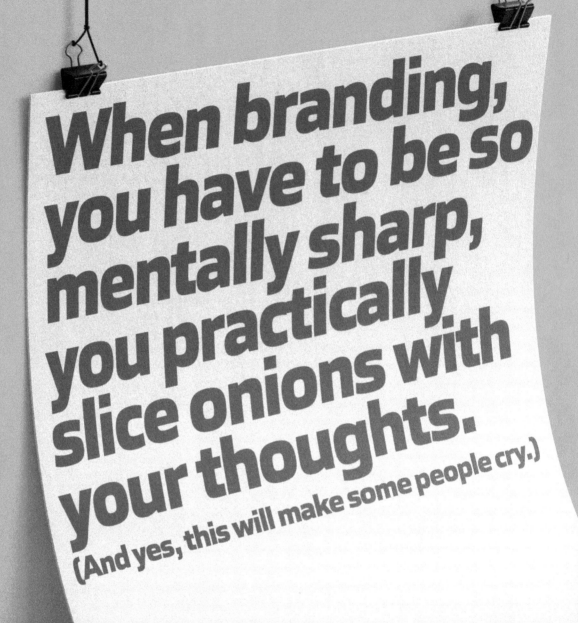

"The difference between the *almost right* word and the *right* word is really a large matter. 'Tis the difference between the lightning bug and the lightning."
Mark Twain, American writer, humorist, entrepreneur, publisher, and lecturer

3

Four words

Of the branding books I'd read, I commonly found 5-8 pages out of the entire book to have the core information with the rest offering little or fluff.

Remember how shocked I was to discover Amazon had over 8,000 branding books? Well this I know: when a specific discipline has that many opinions on one subject, something fundamental is always missing. Always.

The omitted fundamental? A definition and a universal reason for branding. And it came down to four words:

"The art of differentiation."

Now, are you ready to rumble?

"The greatest enemy of knowledge is not ignorance, it is the illusion of knowledge."
Stephen Hawking, noted English theoretical physicist, cosmologist, and author

4

The 66% rule

Fact: there are three phases every customer goes through with your brand.

Most companies use only the first two of these (66%), when in fact there are actually three: the phase that starts **before they buy**, the phase that occurs **during the sale** (or during the use of your product or service) and the last (most overlooked) phase occurring **after the sale**.

And it's this third phase that will either help differentiate you, lock in loyalty, and explode your brand exponentially or keep your brand on a level battlefield competing on price and trivial distinctions.

Why is this so critical?

Because this is when your customer least expects you to do anything more or care anymore since they've paid and checked out. Using only the first two phases is using what is known as the "transactional sales model."

Too many brands use this outdated (and insulting

to customers, especially millennials) "transactional sales model" to drive sales and move product.

There are a number of severe problems with this approach:

- This model considers as its goal the sale, rather than the customer relationship

- It focuses on "moving product" instead of providing amazing value, and

- It merely meets expectations (at best) and never exceeds them.

Worst of all, it ignores the last, least anticipated, and most potentially profitable part of the sales cycle: the actual third phase of the full branding cycle.

It's the difference between having a business and having a brand (fact: when you have a brand, you can do things a run-of-the-mill business can't even contemplate).

This is what separates great brands—Apple, Nordstrom,

Harley Davidson, Nike, Coach and Airbnb—from the rest.

As brands, these companies don't stop at the transaction.

They not only understand the actual transaction doesn't end there but in fact **begins** there.

And this insight revolutionizes how these brands do business, elevating them from **selling** the customer to **wowing** the customer.

And, with this power, impacting how customers perceive them.

So will you choose 100% of the branding cycle or settle for 66%?

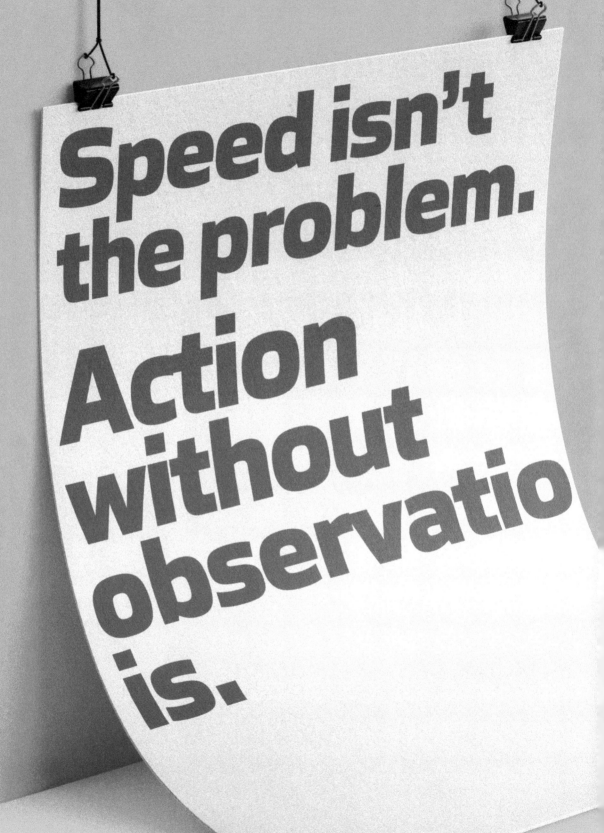

"When something is important enough,
you do it even if the odds are not in your favor."
Elon Musk, Founder of Tesla,
investor, engineer, and inventor

5

Brands think too small

Every brand's goal must include "failing bigger."

In other words, take the bigger risk to truly innovate– for something unbelievable, unimaginable, unanticipated, **and** unstoppable.

It's a combination of bravado, single-minded focus, and intelligent determination aligned to "reality" but **not** molded by it.

Why? Because innovation is the cost of doing business today, not some add-on that gets pulled out when things get rough.

6

The #1 killer of brands

A brand must be visible if it will ever help people. To blend in fails not only your brand but the people it can potentially help.

To become visible, brands must differentiate. Otherwise, a brand puts itself on the same playing field as its competitors.

Here is a branding riddle many companies wrestle with:

"Can any one company use the same words, messages, and promises as other companies **and** convince the world how 'unique' they are?"

The answer: you can't.

The reality here is this is a zero-sum game of clichés where there is no winner.

The same words, the same messages, the same promises as other brands are clichés, and they defeat why your brand exists.

Clichés are marketing's silent killers. Which is why I've been known to say a cliché will kill a brand faster than a roomful of politicians.

Clichés are your brand's enemies, no matter how passionately convincing they may sound.

"There isn't any significant difference between the various brands of whiskey, or cigarettes, or beer. They are all about the same. And so are the cake mixes and the detergents, and the margarines…
The manufacturer who dedicates his advertising to building the most sharply defined personality for his brand will get the largest share of the market at the highest profit."
David Ogilvy, founder of Ogilvy & Mather considered by many "The Father of Advertising"

7

Your first step in Brand Intervention

This is your first step: weeding out any clichés and clarifying how and why you're different. Like anything worthwhile, brands have life injected into them from people like you and me and your next door neighbor, each of whom has some dream they've yet to let loose in the world.

Dreams have life in them. And we already know clichés **will** kill not only your brand but the dreams they're based on.

It's your choice to use clichés or not. It's equally your choice to adopt something that's truly distinct. **And** differentiating. And **so** **inspiring** that it just may change the world.

There's a law you must know: if your brand's using clichés, you're promoting your category, not your brand. Break that law and you break your brand.

"Last night I was lying in bed and I had an idea for an outfit and I just made myself get up and sketch it real fast then went back to sleep. I think it's when you say 'I'm too tired I have to go to bed' is when creativity stops coming. If God calls you, pick up the damn phone."
Stefani Joanne Angelina Germanotta a.k.a. Lady Gaga, American singer, songwriter, and actress

8

A brand is a tool of transformation

As brands, we shift the wandering eye into a focused one, transforming hazy hopes into crystal-clear aspirations.

The mistake is brands too often use transactions as the only worthwhile metric. A transaction is **the result** of the magic that preceded it. **Don't forget the magic.**

The transaction is simple confirmation that the magic, the real value, (the care, compassion, interest, and passion) occurred in the first place.

What adds value in today's world? Speed and efficiency add value. Surprises add value.

Learning something we didn't know adds value. Getting more than we expected **just for the heck of it** adds value.

Uber replaced the outmoded "taxi dispatcher system" since every citizen now had a mobile device. The old dispatcher model ceased adding value in this new world because it was solely based on "operations" and "transactions."

Airbnb disrupted the hospitality industry since hotels and their reservation systems were limited at best and an inconvenience at worst. This new model replaced this old "transaction model" with discovery and a sense of intimacy and adventure.

iTunes disrupted the old model of "record stores" and retail outlets as the distribution channel for music to the consumer. Record stores used to be places were music lovers could go to shop, helped by employees who were **also** music lovers. They talked. Shared musical discoveries. These were replaced by disinterested employees who simply waited to charge your card, often without uttering a single syllable. The magic was gone.

The magic of you and me comes **before** any transaction does.

When that magic (brought about by humans) ceases to exist, so does your brand.

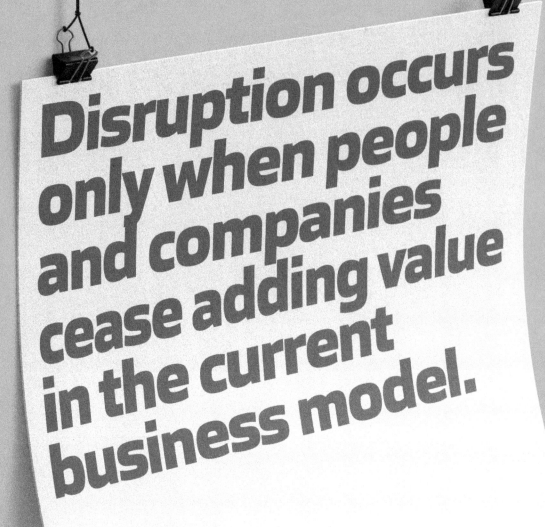

Disruption occurs only when people and companies cease adding value in the current business model.

"If committees told the truth:
... we will compromise the art and the vision out of it,
we will make it reasonable and safe and boring."
Seth Godin, American author, entrepreneur,
marketer, and public speaker

9

Committees never created a great brand

Committees don't work for one fundamental reason: everyone in the room is given equal weight even though their actual experience, knowledge, or track record are anything but equal.

Ignoring this fact, committees become a festival of opinions rather than a review of possibilities—all while sucking the life and potential out of the room faster than a breach in the hull of the USS Enterprise.

One option is to have a small group of 3-4 people with one or two of them having the final authority and decision.

Eliminate the committee. Empower your brand.

"My family could only afford to get me the box of eight Crayola crayons, but I craved the one with all 24 colors. I wanted magenta and turquoise and silver and gold."

Joni Mitchell, Canadian singer-songwriter and painter

10

What to do before you brand

The only thing worse than weak coffee is weak branding.

No brand can afford to be timid or tentative.

Why? Because neither a weak brand nor weak coffee will wake us up (and that's the job of branding).

Neither coffee nor branding work when diluted.

Make sure your brand is bold, standing for something that's worth waking up for.

May your enemies be weak and your coffee strong.

"Only those who attempt the absurd
will achieve the impossible."
M.C. Escher, famous Dutch graphic artist

11

As a brand,
you can't afford
to be selfish

Look around and you'll find something common amongst great brands: they have a "secret mission" of sorts.

Businesses need to be about making the world better, or at least their industry better, not just their own brand and its balance sheets.

Take Apple. Under Steve Jobs, Apple was known for its

computers, mobile devices, and an easier, more intuitive user experience.

But Apple had a bigger scope: empowering the creative individual, not subscribing to the very compromised user experience of the time and not adding to the "corporate beige" junk heap.

So in looking at your business, look at the "small things" you can tackle and the bigger evolution you must impact.

Ask yourself:

- Who can we transform by our product?

- What complacency can we disrupt?

- **What frustration can we transform into a movement to revolutionize how things have been for way too long?**

- **What monopoly can we democratize for an underserved group of people?**

"You say you want a revolution. Well, you know ...
we all want to change the world ... ."
The Beatles

12

Brands are
too timid

Too many brands plan incrementally and are not nimble enough. They take timid steps in an evolutionary way, rather than taking bold steps in a revolutionary way.

Most of the time, this will be found in companies that seek to have a "collective agreement" approach.

Breakthroughs occur under strong leadership not under "group think." Remember, committees are not known for moving things forward nor being the foundation for ingenuity.

Today, no company can afford to operate like a committee.

Lead proudly. Be bold.
Push the limits.

The cautious, evolutionary,
"let's-not-upset-anyone"
approach isn't the approach
we find in winners.

How many lousy paintings did
Picasso throw away before
he did the pieces we consider
legendary masterpieces?

Replace being timid with being smart enough to say "No" when you encounter crap and "Yes" when you're lucky enough to be in the presence of (and quick enough to spot) awesome.

"Different is better when it is more effective or more fun."
Tim Ferris, author of four #1 *NY Times* and *Wall Street Journal* bestsellers

13

Brands are everywhere & forget that

Every brand is in the "tell me why I should care" business.

The reason is simple: because we are all one keystroke away from a million other options than the one we're offering.

Differentiate, if your goal is to grow.

Differentiate, if your goal is to be seen as valuable beyond your price tag.

Differentiate, if you want others to care about your product or service as much as you do.

Differentiate, if you wish to survive.

"What I love about the creative process, and this may sound naive, but it is this idea that one day there is no idea, and no solution, but the next day there is an idea. I find that incredibly exciting and conceptually actually remarkable."
Jonathan Ive, Chief Design Officer at Apple

14

Why I love branding

Branding is a symphony.

It's that perfect moment of silence between the notes. It's that master stroke in the kitchen. It's that pause before that one perfectly delivered line in a script. It's that tagline that cuts through today's glut of gibberish.

No matter how well-written the script, how talented the musicians, how fresh the ingredients, how new the musical instruments, it is ultimately **what we do with them** that transforms them into something magical.

I love that magic.

That symphony of design, color, shape, form, and motion captures people's attention.

It's why I could give two entrepreneurs $100,000 each and one will become a millionaire helping thousands of people and the other will end up a pauper.

It's the magic we each bring.

That's what branding is really all about.

"Others have seen what is and asked why.
I have seen what could be and asked why not."
Pablo Picasso, acclaimed
Spanish painter and sculptor

15

Too many brands are boring

Be the brand that isn't boring and cannot be ignored.

Every brand must ask, "Why should anyone give a damn about our brand?"

Why should anyone care about "our baby," that thing we've sweated over? That's the question we must answer if our goal is to make a difference.

Too few companies look at their brand under this microscope: have we done everything possible to **not** be ignored and **not** be seen as average?

Before you can make a difference, there's a prerequisite: you have to have something worth being heard **when you get that attention.**

That's why social media fails for so many companies. They think, "Let's get a ton of followers" and yet never work out what to say when all of the eyes and ears show up (and then wonder why they all leave).

Your brand's a party. Your dialogue's your refreshment.

When everyone's expecting luke warm pizza, be the one serving amazing seafood, sizzling steak, fresh ingredients, and mouthwatering appetizers to ensure you'll never be predictable or boring.

"No matter what people tell you,
words and ideas can change the world."
Robin Williams, American stand-up
comedian and actor

16

Brands must awaken people

Excite your customer.
Otherwise, your brand is a
sleep aid and a sales killer.

An alert and excited customer
is the best kind. The more
alert and engaged your
customer is, the stronger
your bond.

Uninspired customers and
bored prospects suck (unless

you are **only** there to educate them and not sell them).

The more awake your customers are, the more alive they are, and the more they'll talk about you.

Remember: boredom, complacency, and death are close cousins.

"Great companies start because the founders want to change the world... not make a fast buck."
Guy Kawasaki, best-selling author, Silicon Valley venture capitalist, and one of Apple's employees originally responsible for marketing the Macintosh computer line in 1984

17

Brands must be relevant

No brand can afford to simply arrive. **Be vitally relevant**. Be impossible to ignore.

Use design, language, color, and storytelling to make that connection—that impression and inimitable dent others try to make—to rise above the noise.

Facts, products, services, information, and numbers aren't your brand.

The magic is your brand and achieves so much more.

If you're not igniting passions, dreams, aspirations, and the impulse to change or evolve, **you're not branding**. And not staying relevant.

"Your brand is what other people say about you
when you're not in the room."
Jeff Bezos, Founder, Chairman, and CEO of Amazon.com

18

Brands must do more steering

Currently too many brands are being "driven." They are in a reactionary mode rather than a proactive one.

Proactive means the fire starts with you and remains ignited because you're the spark and the fuel. You're consciously steering the ship.

Reactionary means the spark is "out there," and you're simply reacting to those outside forces.

Choose to look and be observant so you know when to shift gears and accelerate into the passing lane, long before outside circumstances force you to.

"I don't like looking back. I'm always constantly looking forward. I'm not the one to sort of sit and cry over spilt milk. I'm too busy looking for the next cow."
Gordon Ramsay, internationally renowned, multi-Michelin starred chef and TV personality

19

Brands aren't a box...

If your brand is limiting you, it's wrong. Your brand must liberate you.

Brands are a launch pad.

Brands aren't a box where you can't color outside the lines— a box that restricts initiative, prevents fluidity and hampers the ability to swerve nimbly.

The "box idea" is mistaken and limiting. Forget the cliché of "thinking outside the box."

Instead, use the box **as your stage** to dance on, to be a celebration of what your brand's about and where your customer can celebrate the way your brand has aided the quality of their life.

"No amount of great animation will save a bad story."
John Lasseter, Chief Creative Officer of Pixar Animation
Studios, Walt Disney Animation Studios, and
DisneyToon Studios

20

Brands are too close to their own story

Brands are in the storytelling business.

We are here to tell a story that keeps you and me 1) on the edge of our collective seats or 2) has us reaching for the tissues to wipe away the tears.

In other words, as brands, we must step back and

1. Take a look at the Big Picture,

2. Define who our hero is,

3. Establish who is the villain we oppose, and

4. Make an impact.

Ignore this sequence, and you become the villain.

"Value is not determined by those who set the price. Value is determined by those who choose to pay it."
Simon Sinek, British/American motivational speaker, marketing consultant, and author of *Start with Why*

21

Brands cannot confuse price with value

Price is what someone pays. Value is what someone gets.

Every brand must offer more than a good price. The more value you provide, the less price becomes the driver. How could Apple introduce the first iPad, the first tablet introduced to consumers in 2010 (a horrendously bad economic year), with people lining up around the block ready to spend $800 when times are hard? Value.

A cheaper price may inspire a purchase, but it won't inspire loyalty. Why? Because the only value you offer is less impact on someone's wallet. That's less pain, not more gain.

"Size matters not. Look at me. Judge me by my size, do you? Hmm? Hmm. And well you should not."
Yoda, Legendary Jedi Master

22

Why what you do doesn't matter

Your brand is **not** what you do or make. It's what your customer gets that changes their lives for the better.

Every brand must be 100% clear on the difference between **what it makes** (and sells) versus **what its customer buys**.

Porsche makes a car. But customers buy **status in the passing lane**. Häagen-Dazs makes ice cream yet people buy **the ultimate adult indulgence**. Chanel makes a formula. Yet women buy **feeling beautiful**.

Once you know what you're selling, please clarify what your customer is buying.

"Reality leaves a lot to the imagination."
John Lennon, singer, songwriter, Beatle

23

Tell a story

Some brands have "telling the truth" confused with "boring me to death with facts."

Facts are like ingredients to a recipe. They can end up dull and boring or dynamic and exciting depending on who's doing the preparation.

Storytelling is part of branding.

It's the difference between providing "information" and providing "inspiration."

Whoever said facts were meant to be dull was ill-informed.

Use the art of storytelling to keep your customers and prospects engaged.

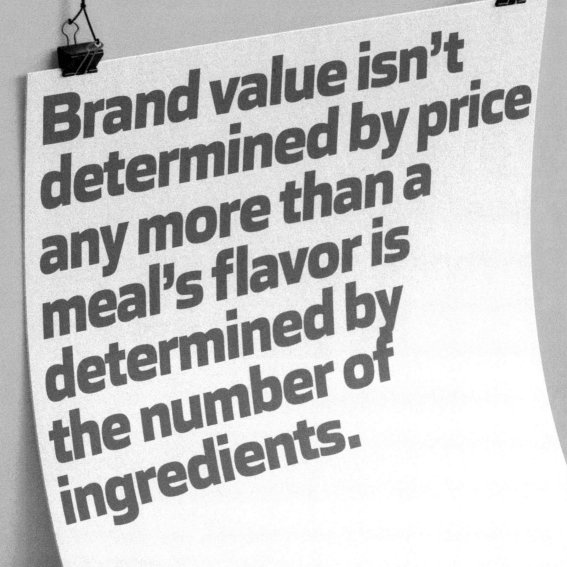

Brand value isn't determined by price any more than a meal's flavor is determined by the number of ingredients.

"If you want to live a happy life,
tie it to a goal, not to people or things."
Albert Einstein, German-born theoretical physicist

24

What the most successful entrepreneurs (and brands) know

I love entrepreneurs.

Who are entrepreneurs?
Oprah Winfrey. Steve Jobs.
Walt Disney. Mark Zuckerberg.
Jeff Bezos. Elon Musk.
JK Rowling. Thomas Edison ...
to name a few.

Entrepreneurs have qualities
that are unmistakable. Much
like the great brands we all
know. My entrepreneurial

clients span the spectrum from global multi-millionaires to serial entrepreneurs and startups to global brands, local brands, and even cities.

The most successful brands share qualities with the greatest entrepreneurs.

The most successful entrepreneurs I know never get satisfied with some random achievement, thus losing sight of their hunger and thirst for the bigger goal. They never confuse an insight with an achievement.

The most successful entrepreneurs I know have a relentless, bottomless persistence that makes others feel like they're being lazy bums.

The most successful entrepreneurs I know are known for their care and passionate interest in others.

The most successful entrepreneurs I know make others wonder if they will ever stop (or if they have a stunt double).

The most successful entrepreneurs I know have an insatiable desire to help, serve, and improve the conditions of others.

Most notably, the most successful entrepreneurs I know **never mistake** an insight–a mere slice–for the whole pie.

And they never take a shortsighted approach to a long-term goal.

The greatest brands of the world share the same traits as today's most successful entrepreneurs.

"A branding program should be designed to differentiate your cow from all the other cattle on the range. Even if all the cattle on the range look pretty much alike."

Al Ries, marketing professional and author of
The 22 Immutable Laws of Branding

25

The problem of branding

As I've stated in this book, brands mistakenly attempt to use the same words (and images and promises) to tell how unique and unlike their competition they are.

The only less effective strategy is insisting on using the same old ineffective strategy because "it's what we've always done."

Confusing busy-ness with effectiveness demonstrates an inability to tell the difference between quantity and quality.

Something that looks terrible on any balance sheet.

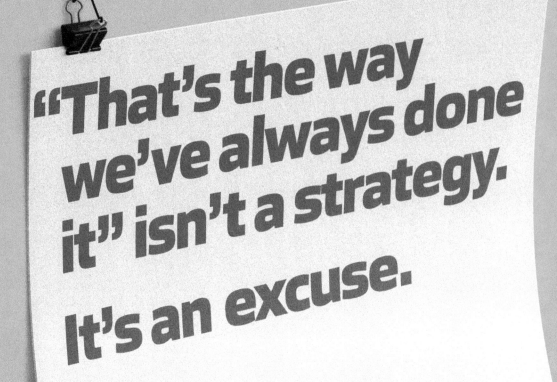

"Good is the enemy of great. And that is one of the key reasons why we have so little that becomes great."
Jim Collins, author of *Good to Great*, and leading American business consultant

26

Good vs. great

A good brand makes us feel good about what **they** stand for.

A great brand makes us feel good about what **we** stand for.

"Fashion is not something that exists in dresses only. Fashion is in the sky, in the street, fashion has to do with ideas, the way we live, what is happening."
Coco Chanel, French fashion designer and businesswoman, creator of Chanel No. 5 perfume

27

The myth of pretty

Making a brand look pretty without addressing its core brand story is like restoring the beauty of a vintage Porsche without anyone ever looking under the hood to discover its transmission is missing.

Remember, I have been a designer for over 30 years as of this writing, working on brands from Revlon and Estée Lauder to *Rolling Stone* magazine to regional and local brands.

So I know (and love) how something good can be made awesome with design and aesthetics—but never at the expense of the brand's core message.

"Relationships are like muscle tissue, the more they're engaged, the stronger and more valuable they become. The ability to build relationships and flex that emotional connection muscle is what makes social so valuable."

Ted Rubin, CMO, author and social influencer

28

Social media,
hit or myth

If you have nothing more than empty, self-serving messages, social media only tells more of the world—faster than ever before—how shallow and one-sided your brand really is.

Channels won't make any message better nor save a brand if you have nothing valuable to say. They won't be the silver bullet that restores brand value.

They won't "connect you with your audience" if you've got nothing to connect with.

With nothing meaningful to say, social media only amplifies—and accelerates—this fact to the rest of the world faster than ever before.

Have a voice first.

"Tell me who your heroes are and I'll tell you how you'll turn out to be."
Warren Buffett, *Forbes* billionaire, CEO of Berkshire Hathaway

29

Every brand is a dichotomy of two opposing forces

Good and evil.

Every brand must stand for **something** inspired, **something** good, **something** worth saving or worth resurrecting. That thing is our audience's hero.

Oftentimes we are all way too busy, forgetting to mention that thing.

At the same time, every brand must equally be about what it's **opposed to**: that thing that's undesirable, less pure, something that's been compromised. This is our audience's enemy.

Be very clear on what you stand for and equally clear on what you're opposed to.

Sometimes the compromise will be the current options, or a stagnant industry, or the category leader. This leaves you to be the David with your slingshot in hand ready to topple the mighty Goliath.

And your shot between the eyes might simply be reminding people of how good it can get.

And what a hero does when faced with evil.

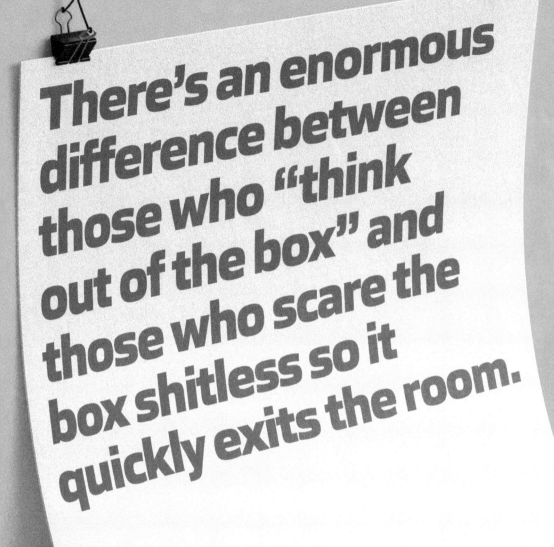

There's an enormous difference between those who "think out of the box" and those who scare the box shitless so it quickly exits the room.

"I've discovered I've got this preoccupation with ordinary people pursued by large forces."
Steven Spielberg, American director, producer, and screenwriter

30

The good and the bad (forget about the ugly)

As I've said, every brand needs to be a protagonist (a hero) of something.

Could be innovation, better taste, cheaper blades, cooler cars, more social activism, greater expression for some group that previously didn't have a voice.

Every brand equally needs an antagonist. Who or what are

you opposing? What bigger industry problem are you solving?

This is an important detail: it's a matter of scope.

If in doubt, go bigger. Get fired up about your brand. Its mission. Its role in the world.

Allow your brand's scope to intimidate you a little.

Then you'll gradually expand to fill that trepidation with confidence, achievement, and boldness.

Why is this important?

Because just by imagining what your next evolution of your brand can be is often terrifying **and** liberating at the same time.

And by expanding to the size of your vision, your triumph will dwarf what previously scared you shitless.

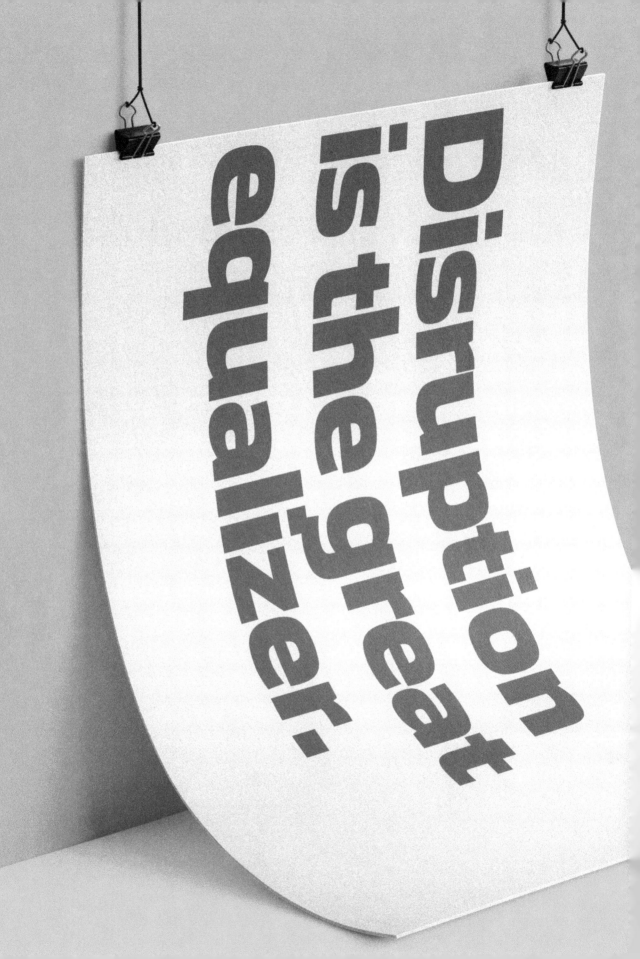

31

Why people shop

People have only two mindsets when shopping—whether it's in a physical store or online, it doesn't matter: the knowns and the unknowns.

The first of these are **the knowns**. The items on their shopping list. The things they already anticipate.

The other list is made up of discovery. These are **the unknowns**. It's the stuff they don't know about, routinely think about, or haven't discovered yet.

It's what makes up "impulse purchases" as well as "new products" or opportunities to make life simpler, faster, tastier, more fun or more convenient.

As a brand, you must balance the two—familiarity (known) and discovery (unknown)—if you plan to really crush it with your brand.

Eliminate "new discoveries" and people will eventually jump ship to go to another brand that does offer them something new. Why? Because today's innovations become tomorrow's mainstays.

The world doesn't stand still.

You can't afford to either.

"We live in an era where the best way to make a dent on the world may no longer be to write a letter to the editor or publish a book. It may be simply to stand up and say something."
Chris J. Anderson, owner of TED (Technology, Entertainment and Design)

32

Consumers demand differences

There comes the crucial point when we need to speak up for what we've created.

So you've created an amazing something.

It fills a need and fires you up. Good.

The next and most vital hurdle is understanding why people buy. You and I choose a brand or product because of one thing: its difference.

"But wait! C'mon David, people buy because of price!" As I've covered in this book, they don't.

Here's how it works. People are faced with choices. This water or that water. This sneaker or that one. This car or computer or smartphone or that one.

It is the job of every brand to clearly establish its point of difference. How it's unlike the other options. How it's really looked at the problem any product or service provides (whether it's speed, convenience, better service, greater experience, higher quality variety, fresher goods, handmade delicacies, faster connections, or simpler one-click checkouts).

That difference equates to value. Worthwhile, quantifiable value.

You know what? Too many brands don't do that job well enough. So what happens?

If you and I fail to clearly and persuasively define and communicate our difference, **the customer will do it for us.**

How?

By first noticing there is "no apparent difference" and then, in order to satisfy that demand for a difference, they will look at the only difference they can isolate: which one's cheaper?

Failing to clearly establish a difference that's valuable (which essentially means they're the same), the only "value" left is "getting the same thing for less."

And (as I've stated in chapter 21), low price only creates

"loyalty" to that lower price point. Not your brand.

There are two lessons to be learned here. The first is that telepathy is **not** a reliable substitute for brand differentiation.

The second is to not make the mistake of thinking people are cheap when they ask which one's cheaper. Realize instead this is simply a blaring signal that your brand has failed to clearly differentiate its value.

Something you can now resolve.

Now you know. Don't make this mistake again.

"We keep moving forward, opening new doors, and doing new things, because we're curious, and curiosity keeps leading us down new paths."
Walt Disney, American entrepreneur, animator, voice actor, and film producer

33

Brands are about the future

I jokingly told a client once what she needed to do with her brand. She responded, "How did you know?"

I said, "It's my job to teleport to the future and return back to report my findings." We both laughed and went on with our conversation. After I hung up, I realized this was more fact than fiction.

Great brands are built backwards: they're built from a future idea of what can be. Such brands fill in the gaps between that future idea and what exists today. Your most valuable resource lies in what's ahead.

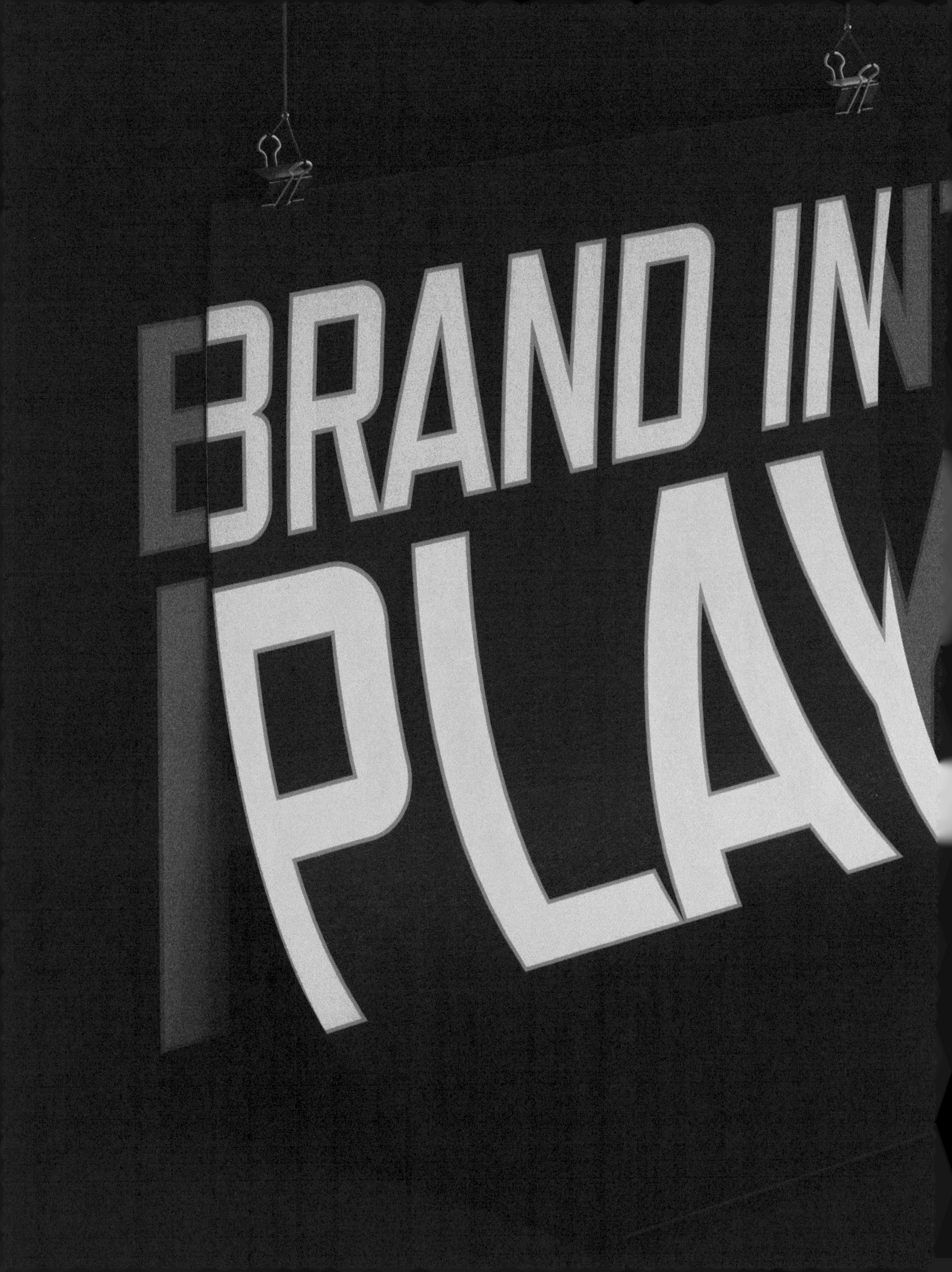
BRAND IN
PLA

ERVENTION
BOOK

You've made it to the Playbook. It's here you'll see how the rules of *Brand Intervention* are played. And the rewards of doing so. At right are some of the companies that have been turned inside out. And on the following pages you get to see (and learn) even more. And then you'll want to re-read *Brand Intervention* from the beginning.

NEW YORK CITY BALLET

equilibrio

Charlie

PORTOFINO
INTERNATIONAL BANK

Steeped in tradition and flavor
THE DAIRY

MENOMONIE
WISCONSIN

RIGHT IN THE MIDDLE OF EVERYWHERE

STUDENT LOAN FREEDOM

TrueFire.com
ignited we stand™

uNdew
SKIN CARE

R&R
REST & RELAXATION BED AND BREAKFAST

DEFIANCE FUEL
defy limitation™

ALCHEMY
GLOBAL

AMERICAN
dance
INSTITUTE

MOVEMENT ON YOUR TERMS

ZERO·NET

WATERFORD

TWENTY **20%** PERCENT

ENZACTA
life. rebuilt.

OSCEOLA
REAL. CHARMING.

CITRON & ROSE
THE NEW TASTE OF
TRADITION

milestone systems

BOTANICAL BAKERY

TOWER
REALTY TRUST, INC

NATURAL. DELECTABLE.
UNAPOLOGETIC.

bead

RELEVANT HABITS
FOR BUSINESS OWNERS

VAO
VAO

BLACK LABEL
PREMIUM
Bean
COFFEE

Making life's occasions fun. It's about time
BigDot Happiness

NATURE'S
GARDEN

free-roam
THE WEDGE
MPLS
CHICKEN
SAUSAGE

free-roam
THE wedge
MPLS
PORK
SAUSAGE

free-roam
THE WEDGE
MPLS
TURKEY
SAUSAGE

free-roam
THE WEDGE
MPLS
BISON
SAUSAGE

free-roam
THE wedge
MPLS
LAMB
SAUSAGE

ORIGINAL DESIGNS
GIFTS YOU CAN FEEL

Avoiding clichés. One day, a startup called my office, a Napa Valley-based company that produced the most amazing shortbread cookies I would ever come to know. It was the owner, Sondra.

After the usual introductory dialog, I asked a series of questions. I knew shortbread cookies were an English treat, a "civilized" cookie. But what Sondra described was something different. Something unorthodox. Something rebellious. My kind of entrepreneur (and cookie). So I said, 'Oh, you're like 'Cookies Gone Wild',' and after we both laughed she said, "That's right."

That opened the door for what were not going to be: predictable, orthodox, or blending in—from design to language to attitude.

The result was that in the first 12 months after this brand intervention, the company saw a 300% increase in sales. The next 12 months? Another 300% increase, totaling a staggering 900% sales increase in 24 months.

True to her slogan, this was certainly an unapologetic— and definitely not a cookie-cutter approach—to branding.

BEFORE

AFTER

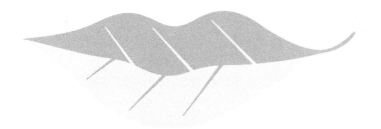

NATURAL. DELECTABLE.
UNAPOLOGETIC.

BAKERY

NATURAL. DELECTABLE.
UNAPOLOGETIC.

Ginger Squared

GARDEN

SHORTBREAD
COOKIES

NET WT 6.5 OZ. (184g)

Realizing the transaction is the start of the relationship.
Joanna Vargas is New York's premier skin care star with a clientele second to none. When Joanna and her husband approached me to elevate their brand, the goal was simple: give customers something amazing when they left the salon. For years, Bloomingdales had set the stage in NYC during the holidays with customers walking around New York carrying one of their iconic bags. This was the inspiration behind this intervention.

The lesson? Never be too proud to know where to look for (and steal) some inspiration.

BEFORE

AFTER

Clearly opposing something. I'd worked with Stu on his previous company's branding. He grew it, sold it, did well, and retired for a full 5 days. Then he started his new company, KnowBe4. The naming concept (to know before something unfortunate happens), the design, and the slogan (Human error. Conquered.) each had to do with his service: Security Awareness Training to protect companies and their employees against hackers—a daily problem costing companies billions in loss and extortion.

Upon starting his new company, Stu first came to me with a name that I promised I would take to the grave. So this intervention started early in the life of this new company. The result is this new brand went from a startup with no sales to an industry leader valued at $100 million in six incredibly fast years.

The lesson? It's like the concept behind this brand intervention: it's never too early to get it right.

Embracing disruption. When Mega Co-op needed to promote its amazing cheese selection to its 82,000 members, there were a number of choices we could make, many of which were predictable. So being a devout foodie, I asked myself what would get my attention?

The answer you see at right. It required me to carve the letters that spelled out CHEESE (yes, I actually did this). No photoshop work or 3D modeling.

To make readers and shoppers stop in their tracks, this needed to be real and authentic. Nothing awakens your customer like a dose of reality that ignores what the competition is blindly embracing.

As a brand grows and builds many points of contact, it becomes necessary to develop what we call a Brand Vocabulary.

The following pages show facets of this vocabulary developed during the brand intervention Mega so enthusiastically embraced for its membership.

HANDMADE
PIZZA

DELICIOSO!

Hot & Tasty

A Slice of Heaven

BORN IN EAU CLAIRE

Mega! CO-OP

Est. 1935

MADE FRESH

RIGHT HERE

TAKE HOME OUR MOIST, SUCCULENT & DELICIOUS

ROTISSERIE CHICKEN

PERFECTION

MOUTH-WATERING

BORN IN EAU CLAIRE

Mega!
CO-OP

Est 1935

Being clear on what customers buy. Steve Griggs is one of New York City's premier landscape designers. When Steve first came to me, my first reaction was, "If you're so damned talented and first-class in what you do, why can't I tell that from the very first moment I see your brand?"

The first detail was to stop pitching homeowners on what he did. Our running joke was, "You save clients headaches, nightmares, marriages, and a shitload of money."

Steve was too close to it. Ask him today, and he'll be the first one to tell you: people now get who he is from the very first moment they see his brand. Now, all the dots connect, all the messages align, and he looks as premier as he is.

BEFORE   **AFTER**

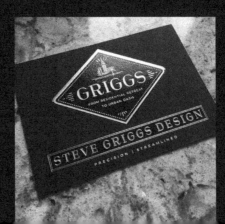

GRIGGS

FROM RESIDENTIAL RETREAT

TO URBAN OASIS

STEVE GRIGGS DESIGN

PRECISION | STREAMLINED

Leading, not following. Mike was hesitant. After 10 months, he finally pulled the trigger on branding his truffles, some of the finest chocolate truffles made in America. This brand intervention involved a total overhaul that defied what all other boutique chocolatiers were doing and everything Mik had done up until that point.

I studied trends others ignored and did a soft launch with the new branding, new brand story, and new box design midsummer. Customers noticed the new box sitting innocently on the back counter. The new branding and new story added immediate value.

How much? Legacy saw a 300% increase in truffle sales in 30 days with no new promotions or flavors, no price changes, and no new sexy personnel. This was followed with posters shown on the next spread.

BEFORE

AFTER

Keeping your brand relevant and nimble. Future Construct started out as a company that leveraged rooftops in Munich for digital satellite dishes. Years later, their business morphed into a company that purchased parcels of land, converting them into above-ground garages and leasing them out. Why? Automobiles are a very valued possession in Germany and there aren't enough garages to go around.

A brilliant business, except for one fact: their brand was out of date in look and language with a (previous) name that no longer applied. Thankfully, the English words, Future Construct, excited their German customers in meaning and concept.

BEFORE   **AFTER**

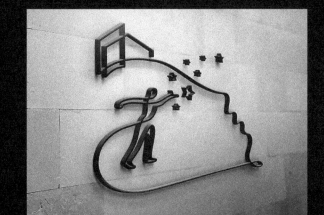

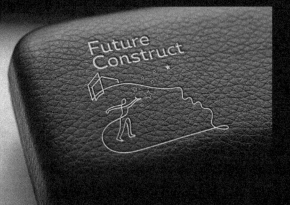

Being about what's next. Branding in other countries is always interesting. One has to get familiar with another culture, their values, and their preferences. Amazingly, it doesn't change any of the principles of brand intervention.

Greenleaves Vitamins is a Netherland-based company whose brand was out of date, blending in with many of the usual clichés common amongst other vitamin manufacturers. The goal of this brand intervention was simple: redefine the brand and its voice so it reflected the future, not the past.

BEFORE

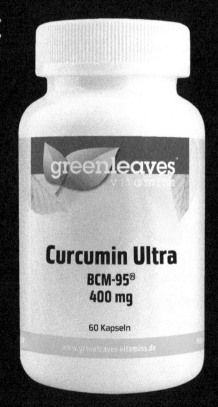

FLOHSAMEN-KOMPLEX
300 g Pulver

(90 Softgel-Kapseln)

pure
inside

greenleaves
VITALSTOFFE

Exceeding expectations. Some brands have true distinctions that make brand intervention easy. In this case, this startup had no more than five 100% natural ingredients with incredible benefits and more anti-oxidants (due to its ingredients) than a truckload of blueberries.

With those attributes, I had to resolve several points: 1) make the new packaging and branding stand out on the crowded shelf and not look like a condom (which the current package looked like), 2) make it clean and simple in appearance to stand out against the noisy meal-replacement bar competition, and 3) differentiate the new brand and its position starting with this killer tagline, "Delicious. Nutritious. Nothing suspicious."

BEFORE

AFTER

GLUTEN-FREE • NON-GMO • NON-DAIRY • VEGAN

CINNAMON ROLL
NATURALLY SATISFIES HUNGER

DELICIOUS. NUTRITIOUS. NOTHING SUSPICIOUS.

NET WT 1.41 OZ. (40G)

GLUTEN-FREE • NON-GMO • NON-DAIRY • VEGAN

COCONUT BROWNIE
NATURALLY SATISFIES HUNGER

DELICIOUS. NUTRITIOUS. NOTHING SUSPICIOUS.

NET WT 1.41 OZ. (40G)

GLUTEN-FREE • NON-GMO • NON-DAIRY • VEGAN

GINGER SNAP
NATURALLY SATISFIES HUNGER

DELICIOUS. NUTRITIOUS. NOTHING SUSPICIOUS.

NET WT 1.41 OZ. (40G)

Embracing the revolution your brand is capable of causing.
Brands are a powerful tool. So when a 70-year old non-profit
came to get a brand overhaul, I was at first hesitant. This
wasn't just any non-profit; it was one of the largest health
non-profits in the U.S.

Would they really let me help them do what they needed to?
And could we get it past the inevitable committee that any
non-profit has as part of its infrascructure? Thankfully, they
were willing to take that journey with me.

This intervention included a new name, a new brand identity,
a new slogan, a new vocabulary—in essence an entirely
new brand.

The new name implied what they did for their clients helping
them to blossom in life. And the new slogan was inspired by
their location: Philadelphia, the home of independence.
Talk about a revolution.

Independence **Grows Here**

BLOSSOM
PHILADELPHIA

BEFORE

UCP United Cerebral Palsy™
of Philadelphia & Vicinity

Life without limits for people with disabilities™

AFTER

BLOSSOM
PHILADELPHIA

Independence **Grows Here**

BLOSSOM
PHILADELPHIA

BLOSSOM
PHILADELPHIA

Independence **Grows Here**

Using design to differentiate and unify. This startup brand was stumbling around like someone on a diet of decaf coffee and luke warm toast. It needed a robust voice so it could stand up to the most potent roasts out there and give back to the community.

Design and words gave it a voice. Purpose gave it relevance. This is brand intervention at its most grounded.

16 oz

20 oz

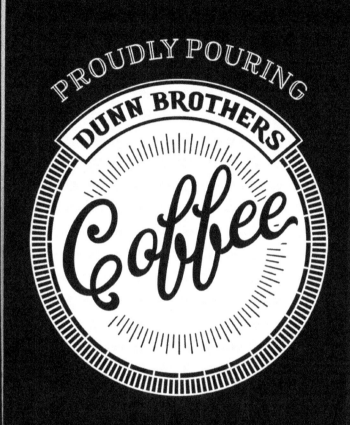

PROUDLY POURING

DUNN BROTHERS

Coffee

TWENTY 20% PERCENT

20% of Net Profits* for Good

Visit *DunnBros.com/dunngood

Conveying what customers buy. Based in Los Angeles, TrendSetters had been delivering market research to a client base that spanned endless industries from startups to companies that had been around. But their brand was cliché and tired.

Looking over what they knew, it was clear they were still selling what they did as a service rather than what their clients were actually buying: answers to business growth.

This brand intervention brought them up to date in a powerful, yet simple way using color, form, concept, an updated company name, and five powerful words as their new slogan.

BEFORE

AFTER

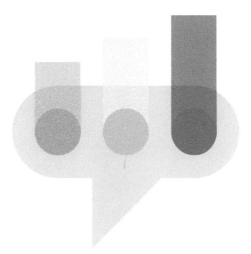

TREND CREATORS
THE ANSWERS TO BUSINESS GROWTH

REBRAND CONCEPT

RESEARCH +
ANSWERS

TREND +
BUSINESS GROWTH

BRAND
IDENTITY

Looking at the bigger picture. When Simply Snackin' approached me, their brand was muddled, hard-to-read, and lacking clarity in the premium jerky space. Premium jerky came along as an alternative to everyday jerky. So, how could Simply Snackin' up their game? In two distinct ways: 1) clean up their act in terms of design, color, and impact and 2) truly differentiate their brand in a compelling way.

How did we achieve the latter? By studying the space they were in and realizing it was *more* than the jerky space: the competition was really the "meal replacement" and the "eating-on-the-go" space which was now heavily crowded with protein bars of every type. The bright idea so they could rise above the noise? "Nature's Original Protein Bar."

BEFORE

AFTER

PLAY HARD  SNACK OFTEN™

SIMPLY SNACKIN'

— NATURE'S ORIGINAL PROTEIN BAR™ —

PLAY HARD SNACK OFTEN™

SIMPLY SNACKIN'
— NATURE'S ORIGINAL PROTEIN BAR™ —

Last word. It's the job of each of us to rescue ideas, dreams, and inspirations *before* they reach the junk heap of compromise and mediocrity.

I hope you join me in this mission.

David@RisingAboveTheNoise.com

I love amazing coffee and inspired espresso.

AN ETHIOPIAN LIGHT ROAST THAT'S
SO SMOOTH, IT MAY CURE SHYNESS

BRAND INTER-VENTION

COFFEE

Maybe someday, I'll create my own coffee brand.

Acknowledgements

Patricia Ross, my editor, for her enthusiasm, rejecting my first efforts, providing the necessary objectivity that enabled me to do what I really needed to do, and making me essentially rewrite the book three times. Your continuous enthusiasm and ownership of how great this book should be kept me going. I am indebted to you.

Daymond John for being like a brother to me and always being gracious, generous, and for first reaching out to me when I wrote my first Shark Tank article for *Fast Company*. That first tweet saying "the best article ever written on Shark Tank" made my decade! And you continue to stay real and authentic regardless of your demanding schedule.

Grant Cardone for being an endless source of inspiration, for never ever stopping in your continuous 10Xing everything you do and touch, and making me feel like I need to raise my game even more.

Ted Rubin for being a kindred spirit in the world of rebelliousness, always telling a good story, and for being inclusive in your life and adventures.

Stu Sjouwerman who is a client, friend, and all-time buddy. You're one of the nicest people in business and in friendship. I am so glad our paths crossed and that we've had time to do some great things. I am looking forward to more.

Steve Olenski for being the "diamond in the rough" brother-from-another-mother who gave me some excellent edits on the final draft, and for always being a helpful freak of nature.

Michael Duff for reading the early proofs, making a few extraordinary catches and recommendations, and for referring to himself with an expletive so I didn't have to.

Sam Hurley (one of the nicest human beings I know) for always being an inspiration of kindness, energy, cheerfulness, and enthusiasm while being busier than (fill in your favorite industrious insect or outdoor animal).

Special thanks to my colleagues David Phillips and Jeroen van Eerden for your continued skill, talent, and competence.

This book is dedicated to all my colleagues and clients around the world I have been honored and fortunate to work with. Your talent and perseverence inspire me. I learn as much from you as I hope you learn from me. This book is dedicated to each of you and your continued success.

And last, but certainly not least, my wife Sherry Brier for being my "rock" who always keeps things in perspective and "getting me" in humor, in astute observation, and in life. So glad to have you by my side in life and living.

CPSIA information can be obtained
at www.ICGtesting.com
Printed in the USA
BVHW020223100719
552849BV00062B/1964/P